THE ELEPHANT BOOK

For the ELEFRIENDS Campaign

Philip Cayford

by

IAN REDMOND

CANDLEWICK PRESS
CAMBRIDGE, MASSACHUSETTS

DEDICATED TO THE AFRICAN ELEPHANT
AND THOSE WHO ARE FIGHTING FOR ITS SURVIVAL

First Candlewick edition 2001

Library of Congress Cataloging-in-Publication Data

Redmond, Ian.
The elephant book : for the Elefriends campaign / by Ian Redmond.
p.   cm.
Originally published: Woodstock, N.Y. : Overlook Press, 1991.
ISBN 0-7636-1634-6
1. African elephant. I. Elefriends (Organization). II. Title.
QL737.P98 R438 2001
599.67'4—dc21   2001029509

2 4 6 8 10 9 7 5 3 1

Printed in Hong Kong

This book was typeset in OPTICather, ATArta, and Hadfield.

Candlewick Press
2067 Massachusetts Avenue
Cambridge, Massachusetts 02140

visit us at www.candlewick.com

The author and publishers wish to thank all of those who gave quotes for the book.
Some appeared in earlier publications as listed below, but most were given to ELEFRIENDS
at the time of its launch in 1989 or during the preparation of this book.
Page 13 Heathcote Williams, *Sacred Elephant*, Cape 1989; page 25 Charles F. Holder, *The Ivory King*, Scribners 1866;
page 27 Cynthia Moss, *Elephant Memories*, Elm Tree Books 1988; page 28 Dr. Iain Douglas-Hamilton, *Among the Elephants*, Collins 1975;
page 31 Dr. Joyce Poole, *Animal Kingdom*; page 38 Dr. S. Keith Eltringham, *Elephants*, Blandford 1982;
page 38 Captain Richard Meinertzhagen, *Kenyan Diary*, 1903; page 43 map after IUCN.

Front cover: **Oxford Scientific Films** Richard Packwood;
Back cover: **Bruce Coleman Limited, Jonathan Scott/Planet Earth Pictures, Oxford Scientific Films** Richard Packwood;
Endpapers: **Visions Photo Inc.**

Contents

Preface by Daphne Sheldrick 4

Introduction 6

The Architect of Africa 8

Trunks and Tusks 10

The Senses 12

Tail, Skin, and Feet 14

The Savannah 16

The Forest 18

The Desert 20

The Water Hole 22

The Salt Diggers 24

The Matriarch 26

Peaceful Bachelors and Battling Bulls 28

The Courtship 30

Birth 32

Early Years 34

Adolescence 36

The Daily Round 38

Death 40

Eviction 42

The Ivory Trade 44

Peaceful Coexistence 46

Final Word About ELEFRIENDS and Index 48

MY HOME in Nairobi National Park, Kenya, has become an orphanage for baby elephants. I have been looking after orphaned wild animals for forty years, but things have been getting worse for the elephants. Little calves are brought to me after they have witnessed their mother die in a hail of machine-gun bullets and the tusks hacked out of the still warm faces of their family. It is hardly surprising they are so hard to save—elephants are sensitive animals.

The orphans go through an intense period of grieving—from one to four months—when we must help them regain the will to live. They need intensive care—huge bottle feeds every three hours, day and night, and constant physical contact to replace their mother's tenderness. Through this work, I have come to know elephants intimately—more so, I think, than anyone else alive—not just in the wild, but as a foster mother to their orphaned young of all ages. My helpers and I have nursed them through their nightmares and slept with them in their straw beds. We have given them the will to live and to return to the wild, under the guidance of Eleanor, one of my first orphans, who now lives free in Tsavo National Park. But our work will not end until every consumer of ivory becomes an ELEFRIEND. Only then will the poaching stop and the babies be left in peace to grow up among elephants—where they belong.

Saving the world's elephants *must* be the responsibility of all thinking people. Every piece of ivory is a haunting memory of a once-proud and majestic being, who has loved and been loved and was part of a close-knit and caring family similar to our own, but who has had to suffer and die in unspeakable agony to yield its tusks for trinkets and ornaments. That is a high price to pay for ivory, and the world should want no part of it. We *can* replant forests, and even reclaim deserts in time, but no one, when the last elephant has gone, can make another.

Daphne Sheldrick.

"The death of an elephant, for me, is like the death of a human being. Elephants, too, feel pain and grief, are kind and compassionate, love their young, and defend their territory against invaders. If we are indifferent to the slaughter and annihilation of this wise and wonderful animal, in order that we may buy ornaments or festoon ourselves with jewelry made from its teeth, we will have taken another irreversible and shameful step toward our own physical and spiritual destruction."

Virginia McKenna, ELEFRIENDS

Philip Cayford

"Until we recognize what the real treasures of the world are, until we learn to share this earth with all its other inhabitants, we will find only temporary

There is an old saying that you cannot share an acre with an elephant. In the new millennium, this truth will determine how many elephants we humans allow to share Earth with us. As more and more people stake their claim for a patch of land on which to grow their crops and raise their

Ian Redmond

families, the elephants that once roamed over Africa and Asia are being squeezed out. Not so long ago, however, there were very real fears that there wouldn't be any elephants in most of their former range. They were being exterminated for a quick profit.

In 1989 the world finally woke up to what was happening in Africa. Elephant numbers had plummeted from an estimated 1.3 million in 1979 to 609,000 in just ten years. The main cause was poaching for ivory. Up to 10,000 elephants were being slaughtered every year, their front teeth hacked out, their bodies left to rot, their tiny calves left to die of starvation. If nothing had been done, the downward curve on the population graph would have hit zero early in this century. The unthinkable was suddenly being talked about—extinction. But this was not news to everyone; the signs had been there for a long time.

It was in 1980 that I became really hooked on elephants. In Kenya that year, I joined an Operation Drake project to build a tourist path up to Kitum Cave in the Mount Elgon National Park, and to monitor the cave for elephants. After witnessing a herd of elephants feeling their way by moonlight into the black maw of Kitum Cave, I knew that I had to find out more about this little-known phenomenon.

Happily, ivory poaching was not then a problem at Elgon, and for several years I did not fear unduly for these elephants because the mining activity wears down the tusks to mere stumps. It seemed to me unlikely that ivory poachers would risk the dangers of hunting in cold, wet rain forest patrolled by park guards for such poor-quality ivory. I was wrong. Such was the demand for ivory around the world that even the scratched and pitted tusks of the Elgon elephants were considered profitable. In 1987, I returned to Elgon to investigate reports of poaching.

As I approached Kitum Cave, the stench of death reached me. There on the forest floor lay the mutilated carcass of a twelve-year-old bull. A seething mass of maggots spilled out from the thick, brown skin; the skull was cut in a single plane—the work of a chain saw. Nearby were the decomposing remains of a three-year-old calf from the same attack. They had been ambushed in the mouth of the cave. Standing there I felt an enormous surge of anger and sadness.

Ivory is not a rock or a wood. It is a dead elephant's tooth. And as long as there is a demand for the ivory earrings, bangles, statuettes, and knickknacks that adorn the wealthy and their homes, someone is going to go out and kill elephants to get a share of that wealth. It is impossible to protect every wild elephant all of the time, but the need for such intensive protection would evaporate if ivory lost its value. And ivory would lose its value if none of us would buy it.

Attitudes have changed in many parts of the world. In May 1989 Tanzania was the first nation to propose a ban on the ivory trade, and the ELEFRIENDS campaign was launched in London. Kenya's President Daniel arap Moi bravely burned 13 tons of confiscated ivory—proving to the world that he was serious about ending the ivory trade. And in October 1989, the nations in CITES (the United Nations Convention on International Trade in Endangered Species) voted to ban the international trade in ivory. This ban has been repeatedly challenged by a handful of southern African

Will Travers

countries but supported by the majority of the thirty-seven African and thirteen Asian countries with elephants. In 2000, a new system of Monitoring the Illegal Killing of Elephants (MIKE) was introduced to provide facts for future debates on whether a limited legal ivory trade leads to an increase in poaching. But the lesson from the past is clear. Poaching is driven by demand, and we-can all help to reduce the demand for things made from elephants' teeth. Please take a

Jonathan Scott/Planet Earth Pictures

personal pledge never to buy or use ivory in any form. And please complain if you ever see ivory on sale. By these simple means, we can all be an ELEFRIEND and help to make the world a safe place for elephants.

"We've had Save the Whale. Now it is time for Save the Elephant."

Dr. Iain Douglas-Hamilton, Nairobi

"Blackened tusks formed the splintered and charred backdrop to a crescent moon of, as yet, unmarked ivory. To some, it may have seemed like a glimpse into an elephant hell, but for me it was not the fire of destruction but one of hope."

Will Travers, Nairobi

Hugo Van Lawick/Nature Photographers Ltd

A MAGNIFICENT bull elephant strides slowly across the savannah. Suddenly he stops to listen, ears spread like sails as if to assist his passage over the sea of grass. What he hears are the deep rumblings of other bulls, or perhaps a female telling him she is ready to mate. Whatever the message, it is carried across the bush by low-frequency sounds, well below the level of human hearing. It wasn't until 1986 that scientists learned that there is more to elephant talk than meets the human ear.

This discovery served to remind us that there is still much to learn about elephants. They play a central role in the ecology of Africa, and many other species of animals and plants could not survive without them.

"The thought of Africa without elephants is appalling."
Sir David Attenborough

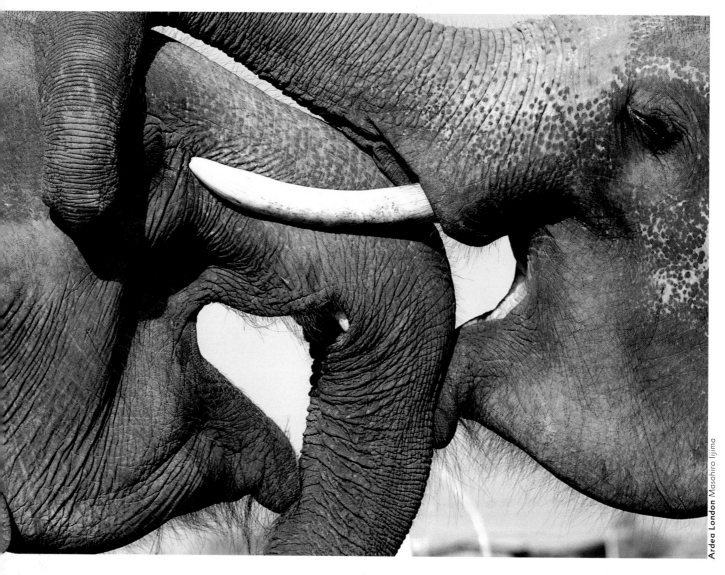

Ardea London *Masahiro Iijima*

Mike Mockler/Swift Picture Library

A N ELEPHANT'S face is unlike any other in the animal kingdom. It has only two front teeth, and these stick out to form the tusks, which continue to grow throughout the elephant's life—except for those of the female Asian elephant (*above left*), which remain small and largely hidden. An elephant uses its tusks both as weapons—in threat displays and actual combat—and as tools—for digging up roots or mineral-rich earth, for stripping bark, and for lifting things with the aid of its trunk.

Ian Redmond

𝒯HE ELEPHANT'S nose and upper lip have become fused and extended to form a novel kind of fifth limb. The Swahili word for trunk is "mkono," meaning hand, because the trunk is used to hold and manipulate things. As a hand, however, it is unique, being equipped with an acute sense of smell as well as touch, and no bones. The lack of bones means that a trunk can bend, fold, or curve in any direction. It is controlled by about 100,000 muscles that

tip. An African elephant's nostrils emerge at the tip of the trunk between two flexible "fingers." So precise is the movement of these trunk fingers that an elephant can delicately wipe a piece of grit from its eye or pick up a single seed from the ground.

The trunk also serves as an early warning system, ever alert to a whiff of danger. If an elephant senses the presence of humans or other predators, it holds its trunk aloft like a nasal

AN ELEPHANT does not perceive the world in the same way that we do. Sight, which for humans is the sense that tells us most about our surroundings, comes a poor third for elephants, behind the senses of smell and hearing.

In proportion to its body size, an elephant's eye seems rather small, being about the same size as a human eye. The iris is normally brown, but it is often hard to see because it is shaded by a very impressive set of eyelashes that sweep out from the upper eyelid. With its eyes placed on either side of its head, an elephant—like a horse—has an almost all-around field of vision, with only a small area directly in front where the sight of both eyes overlaps. But the retina in an elephant's eye has far fewer light-sensitive cells than a human eye, and so its sight is rather poor— particularly in bright light

Ardea London P Morris

and at distances of more than about thirty paces.

Elephants can hear a remarkably wide range of sounds, from the tiny high-pitched squeaks and chirps that they apparently make with their trunks, to the powerful infrasonic rumbles with which they communicate over great areas of bush.

The size of the outer ear, however, has less to do with hearing than with temperature control. When an elephant flaps its ears—or stands into the wind with

Ian Redmond

ears held out to catch the breeze—the moving air takes away excess body heat. The ears are equipped with a network of large blood vessels that act like radiator pipes. These blood vessels give out heat, and as a result, the blood *leaving* the ear vessels is several degrees cooler than when it entered them. This may be why the Asian elephant—which dwells more in shady forests—has smaller ears than the African species, and why the African forest elephant, in its turn, has much smaller ears than the African bush elephant.

Ian Redmond

Between the eye and the ear of an elephant lies the temporal gland—visible as a small, slitlike opening from which a dark fluid often trickles. Behind the slit is a large gland—weighing up to three and a quarter pounds in a bull elephant—whose function is not fully understood. In Asian elephants, temporal fluid only flows from a male in "musth" (*see page 28*), but it often flows in both sexes of the African elephant for no obvious reason. When an African bull *is* in musth, however, his temporal glands swell and secrete a darker, oily fluid, which he rubs on vegetation as a scented signpost to advertise the fact that he is in musth.

"The shape of an African elephant's ear is the shape of Africa. The shape of an Indian elephant's ear is the shape of India. . . . As if Nature had kept an ear to the ground when listening to the elephant's territorial requests."

Heathcote Williams, *Sacred Elephant*

*T*HE LONGEST hairs on an elephant's body are those on the top and bottom of its tail. Each hair is like a thick, glossy black wire, up to two and a half feet in length.

Bruce Coleman Limited *(left and middle)*

*E*LEPHANT SKIN feels rough to a human hand, but this does not mean that it is insensitive. Beneath the tough, horny outer layer there are touch receptors that can pinpoint an irritating insect— to be brushed off by a precise swing of the trunk or, at the rear, by a flick of the tail.

The folds and wrinkles in the skin serve to trap moisture, which slowly evaporates to cool the elephant.

The texture of an elephant's skin varies, from the thick, calloused folds of the forehead to the soft, thin pliable skin behind the ears and under the belly.

$\mathcal{T}$HE SOLES of the feet are thickened into ridges, like the cleats on the sole of a climbing boot. This gives elephants a good grip when negotiating the steep cliffs and slopes that they climb with such surprising ease.

Elephants walk on the tips of their fingers and toes.

Oxford Scientific Films G I Bernard

Bruce Coleman Limited

"The elephant intrigues me so much, its strength and dignity, its silent movement and sudden trumpeting fury, the humor of its young, the threatening beauty of its tusks, the delicate touch of its trunk, and the intelligent look in its wise old eye — all these enthralled me."

the late George Adamson

Inside each foot, the digits rise from the nails on the outside to meet the wrist or heel bones; these rest on a fibrous pad, inside the foot, that acts as a kind of shock absorber.

There are usually five nails on the forefoot, which is round, and four on the more oval-shaped hind foot. When an elephant "kneels" on its front legs, it is actually resting on its wrists; the true knees (with kneecaps) are found only on the hind legs, as in humans. When an elephant stands at rest, the bones in each limb stack to form the sturdy columns that bear up to six and a half tons of elephant!

Heather Angel

*T*HE MOST familiar habitat for African elephants is the savannah, or bush, a vast expanse of rolling grassland dotted with flat-topped acacia trees and divided by winding strips of riverine forest. It is familiar because, of all the elephant habitats, it is the most accessible.

During the rainy seasons, when the grass is green and growing, elephants can be found all across the savannah, tearing up great tussocks with their trunks, beating away the soil, and shearing off unwanted roots with a grind of their molars. Later, when the rains end and the grass yellows and dries, they spend more time in the patches of woodland along river banks. Here the ground is moist and the trees, with their deeper roots, remain green for longer and provide nourishing browse.

Ian Redmond

*T*HE FOREST elephants of Africa are usually the forgotten elephants. Little is known of their behavior, and they are seldom photographed or filmed. And yet some estimates put the number of elephants within the rain forests at 200,000 — about half the continental total.

The true forest elephant is now considered to be a new species, *Loxodonta cyclotis*. It has smaller, more rounded ears, downward-pointing brownish-yellow tusks, and is smaller than the more familiar bush elephant, *Loxodonta africana*. These differences seem to be adaptations to a forest life where, for example, large sweeping tusks would be a disadvantage when pushing through undergrowth.

Ian Redmond

*T*HE ECOLOGICAL importance of elephants cannot be overstated. If the rain forest is seen as a life-generating machine, then the elephant is one of its main cogs. One-third of the many tree species in West African forests rely on elephants to eat their fruit and thereby disperse their seeds in the dung. Some tree seeds will not germinate *unless* they have been passed through an elephant's gut and been deposited in the rich package of manure that is an elephant's dung ball.

Ian Redmond

"A fully grown elephant has little to fear from other animals. He is their essential friend, he makes their roads, he digs their water in dry sand river beds, and he scatters seeds to regenerate the land. Who are we to say he must die?"

the late Bill Travers

SOMETIMES there may not be enough light for the seedling to grow. But when a passing elephant pushes over a nearby tree, breaking the forest canopy and creating a glade, life-giving sunlight can reach the ground and the seedlings will start to grow. Ground-level herbaceous plants grow rampantly in such sunny patches, providing food for forest antelopes and enriching the habitat.

"Let's do it! Let's stop buying ivory, let's stop selling ivory. We can all of us — each one of us — do that."

Bruce Coleman Limited

AMONG the creeping, wind-blown sand dunes or the parched, thorny scrub of the Huab Desert in Namibia, the last thing one might expect to see is a water-loving animal such as an elephant. But like people, elephants have the ability and intelligence to modify their habitat. This enables them to live in the arid conditions of the Huab and other African deserts. Despite the desiccated vegetation and low annual rainfall, elephants survive in these areas because they can dig down in dry river beds to reach water.

The water may be as much as six and a half feet below the surface, but with tusks and trunk, an elephant can excavate a deep seep hole and then wait patiently for it to fill before lifting each trunkful of the precious liquid to its mouth.

Knowledge of the best places to dig for water is handed down from generation to generation. As such, it is a form of "elephant culture," and each separate population of desert elephants has its own unique traditions.

In the same way that human tribes benefit from the knowledge of previous generations, elephants, too, increase their chances of survival. If the last desert elephant were to die, this cultural knowledge would also disappear, and it is unlikely that any future elephants, reintroduced from elsewhere, could succeed without it.

David Back/ICCE

$\mathcal{E}$LEPHANTS are seldom found very far from water. Every day they make their way down to a river, lake, or forest pool to drink. The arrival is usually a leisurely affair, as smaller groups within the herd enter the water in their own time.

After the elephants have quenched their thirst, there is then time to bathe and relax. Their dusty, quilted skins are dunked and showered and liberally plastered with mud. And while there is a serious side to this activity—keeping their skin cool and moist under the hot African sun—it also offers a great opportunity for elephantine fun. Calves wriggle, wrestle, and roll in the mud, emerging like chocolate-coated elephants to challenge their playmates. Even adults seem to drop all dignity at times and act plain silly, throwing trunkfuls of water around like overgrown schoolboys.

Ian Redmond

Ian Redmond

Ꜫ LEPHANTS, like all other animals, need salt. If their food does not contain enough, they will search until they find a salt lick, an outcrop of mineral-rich strata. But unlike the other salt-hungry animals, elephants cannot actually lick the salt. Their tongues are simply not long enough to reach around their trunks and tusks. Instead, they dig it up. Using their tusks like a spade to loosen the earth, elephants pick up the clods with the delicate tip of their trunks and put them into their mouths. Even rocks, if they are salty, are ground up by the massive molars and swallowed.

"Hindoo mythology teaches that the earth is supported by eight elephants. . . . In the Ramayana is a very curious account of the journey of a party of men who penetrated to the interior of the earth, and had an audience with the famous elephants."

Charles F. Holder,
The Ivory King

Ian Redmond

ℰLEPHANT salt-digging behavior has undercut cliffs in some parts of Africa and Asia, but in only one place has it resulted in large caves—on Mount Elgon in Kenya.

In the dark recesses of these huge caverns, elephants feel their way to traditional mining bays deep underground. There, working only by touch, they use their tusks as living ivory chisels to pry off lumps of sodium-rich volcanic ash to eat. From their earliest days, baby elephants accompany their mothers right into the caves. The cows, however, keep a careful trunk on their offspring to prevent them wandering off and falling down a crevasse or rock face in the pitch-dark interior.

*T*HE LEADERSHIP of a family herd of elephants always rests with a venerable old female, known as the matriarch. The herd she leads normally consists of her daughters and grand-daughters, with perhaps one or two sisters and their offspring as well. These interrelated females coop-erate in raising their young, even to the extent that one elephant mother will some-times suckle another's baby.

When danger threatens, all the family members turn to the matriarch for guidance. Her behavior, based on decades of experience, will tell them whether to fight or flee. She may lead them to form a defensive circle, with the calves safely inside and the adults facing outwards, ears spread and heads held high to increase their apparent size and intimidate the foe.

If members of a family become separated, they appear anxious and try to keep in

Mark Boulton/ICCE

touch with long-distance calls, called "contact rumbles." When they come together again, they go through a special greeting ceremony that involves rumbling, trumpeting, urinating, and defecating in a tight ring, with heads and tails held high. This greeting is reserved for closely related individuals, and so when two different

families meet and greet with excitement, it usually means that some of the elder cows are relatives who grew up together and have kept in touch over the years. Few animals other than humans live in such a complex social network, where the relationships span decades rather than years or months.

"After eighteen years of watching elephants I still feel a tremendous thrill at witnessing a greeting ceremony. . . . I have no doubt even in my most scientifically rigorous moments that the elephants are experiencing joy when they find each other again. . . . it is elephantine joy and it plays a very important part in their whole social system."

Cynthia Moss,
Elephant Memories

$\mathcal{T}$HE MATRIARCH will not allow adult bulls to live within the family unit on a regular, day-to-day basis. When one of the females comes into estrus, however, and is ready to mate, bulls can often be seen hanging around the outskirts of the herd, displaying their strength and vying for her attentions.

Ian Redmond

*O*NCE THEY reach maturity, bull elephants spend most of their time alone or with other bulls. They may form loose associations with other males, but these bachelor herds are not based on long-term social bonds like those of females. One or two young bulls are sometimes seen with a very old tusker—which led the white hunters to dub them "askaris"—meaning soldiers or guards. Their presence would certainly help to thwart an attack by a trophy hunter or ivory poacher (to the elephant the difference is irrelevant), but it may be the young bulls who benefit most from the relationship. The older, more experienced bull passes on his knowledge of "elephant politics" and how to survive adverse conditions such as drought.

Male elephants indulge in frequent trials of strength called sparring. These mock fights serve to establish a hierarchy based mainly on size and strength. Because elephants have such good memories, they not only recognize the other males they come across but also know their relative social standing without having to fight to re-establish it whenever they meet.

The one thing that regularly disrupts this organized male society is the onset of musth. African bulls only begin to show musth in their midtwenties, and only for a short time each year. It is a period of risk taking when they rush around with heads held high, challenging other bulls, secreting from their temporal glands, giving special low-frequency musth rumbles, and leaving behind them a trail of strong-smelling urine wherever they wander.

Bruce Coleman Limited

Ian Redmond

"In their response to danger, every bull usually looks after himself, which makes it all the more remarkable that bulls do sometimes help others that have been wounded."

Dr. Iain Douglas-Hamilton,
Among the Elephants

OTHER, MORE dominant males may even back down from a younger male in musth. As they get older the musth period becomes longer and more regular, but it is always a drain on the bull, because so little time is spent feeding. However, for most of the year the bulls feed quietly and spar good-naturedly to build up their strength for this all-out period of fighting and mating. A fight between two musth bulls is one of the most impressive sights in nature, and may sometimes be a fight to the death.

WHEN A BULL elephant passes through a family herd, he is alert to the subtle scents of the females. A female elephant is in estrus—able to conceive—for only a few days each year and so the bull reaches out his trunk and then curls it to a special organ in the roof of his mouth to test whether any of the cows are receptive. If one is, she might move off with head held high, inviting him to chase her and giving low sexy rumbles. She will run fast and not stop for young bulls, but for a big dominant bull she will slow down after a time, allowing him to catch up and lay a gentle trunk across her back.

"The maneuvering of the males around an estrus female is like a well-choreographed dance in slow motion; each step the female takes is mirrored by the musth male."

Dr. Joyce Poole,
Animal Kingdom

FEMALE elephants do seem to choose whom they mate with, and usually show a clear preference for a large musth bull in his prime—between thirty-five and forty-five years of age. He will try to stay with her as a consort and guard her against other males until the end of her estrus, when conception occurs.

To avoid too great a crush on his partner, the bull will lightly rest his tusks and forefeet along her back when mating, but he will take most of his weight on his own hind legs. Afterward, the female gives a series of low calls, which prompts her family to join her in what is termed a mating pandemonium. All the females rumble, scream, trumpet, urinate, defecate, and secrete from their temporal glands in a contagious frenzy of activity that presumably advertises the presence of an estrus female to any other males within earshot. As each bull arrives, he inhales the exciting scent of estrus, while she extends a welcoming trunk to investigate his state of musth. To mate, however, he has to separate her from her consort—a system that ensures it is the biggest and most powerful bull who finally fathers her next calf.

THE BIRTH of a baby elephant is an event of great interest to all in the family herd. The new mother is usually attended during labor by another cow—the "midwife"—as she moves restlessly and prepares herself for the birth.

With a gentle nudge from its mother, a newborn calf can usually wobble to its feet within half an hour of birth, but it is totally dependent on her for food, protection, and instruction. A baby elephant's sense of security comes from within a palisade of huge pillar-like legs; reassurance is the gentle caress of a trunk. Until one year of age, a calf can take shelter beneath the rumbling girth of its mother's chest. There too, between the cow's front legs, it will find sustenance.

To feed, a baby elephant reaches upward, curls its funny little trunk onto its forehead, and drinks, sucking with the mouth, not the trunk.

A female elephant has breasts similar in size and shape to those of a woman, except that the nipples are angled sideways, making them easier for the baby to reach as it stands at her side. The mother, by simply moving one leg forward, can continue to reach for her own food while her calf feeds.

P. C. Lee

Richard Packwood

"The elephant is a symbol of much that we aspire to ourselves — strength, dignity, wisdom, humor, and close family ties. We owe it to our children and to the elephant himself, to reverse in the twenty-first century the tide of destruction that swept through Africa during the twentieth century."

Philip Cayford, Wildlife filmmaker

THE BABY is born after a twenty-two-month gestation period—the longest in the animal kingdom. Births can occur at any time of the year, but there is a peak in numbers during the rainy season, when there is a rich supply of fresh green vegetation for nursing mothers. This peak occurs because the biggest breeding bulls time the onset of their musth to coincide with the rains, thereby giving their calves the best chance of survival when they are born nearly two years later.

Although a single calf is the norm, twins are occasionally born, and both calves may survive if food is plentiful.

YOUNG elephants are filled with an insatiable curiosity about their surroundings. The main organ of exploration is, of course, the trunk. But for the first few months, baby elephants have no idea how to control that appendage. With their oversized ears and undersized trunks, they look and behave more like cartoon characters than real elephants. Less-than-impressive threat displays are directed at all and sundry—even butterflies or birds—but if anything threatens *it*, the calf is quick to scuttle back to its mother. The calves have a lot to learn. Like humans and apes, elephants have a long childhood during which they absorb the knowledge of their elders. The strongest bond in elephant society is that between a mother and her calf. A male calf is more

demanding and the mother usually gives in to his tantrums. She suckles him more often and he grows faster than his sisters. But both sexes soon learn that they must keep up when, for example, it is time to leave the waterhole. If they lag behind, there is always an aunt or a sister to lend a friendly helping trunk.

While their mothers are feeding, much of the calves' time is spent in roughhouse play with their friends—favorite games being Push of War and Climbing on Top of Your Playmate.

"Once the matriarchs are gone, who will teach the orphans the greeting rumble and who will be left for them to greet?"

Dr. Joyce Poole,
Animal Kingdom

Ian Redmond

THE DIFFERENCES in the behavior of male and female calves become more marked as young elephants approach adolescence. Sexual maturity in both sexes comes between eight and thirteen years of age, but social maturity is different. A cow is likely to give birth to her first calf during her early teens, with the support and reassurance of her mother and aunts. A bull, on the other hand, is unlikely to father any offspring until he is in his thirties and is able to compete with older, more dominant males.

For the males, the boisterous games of calfhood gradually develop into the more serious sparring of young bulls. The forests ring with the clack of ivory on ivory as they fence with their tusks, and trials of strength are settled by head-on shoving matches and bouts of trunk wrestling.

Once the rapidly growing bulls begin to take an interest in estrus females, they are ejected from the family herd by the matriarch and spend a decade building up their strength and experience before the first signs of musth appear, and the prospect of success in courtship.

"The elephant is in a class by itself. And yet hundreds of elephants are killed so people can wear ivory bracelets. This is wrong. The elephant is a treasure to the world, and the world must protect this treasure."

the late
James Stewart,
Actor

AS FEMALE calves grow up, they grow out of play-fighting games and begin to take on some of the duties of looking after the younger babies in the herd. Calves are usually weaned during their third year, and the interval between births is about five years. This means that as the second calf begins to explore, an older sister (or cousin, if the first baby was female) is on hand to help. This

nursemaid role of the young females is of great importance to both animals. The nursemaid gains by learning some of the skills of motherhood, and the smaller calf gains by increased protection and a greater sense of security. If a mother dies after her young calf has been weaned, the calf is far more likely to survive if a nursemaid is on hand to look after it.

"To be within a few feet of a group of sleeping elephants at night is a profoundly moving and peaceful experience. . . . Few other animals would dare to abandon themselves to such luxuriously profound slumber in the dangerous African bush."

Dr. S. Keith Eltringham, *Elephants*

Richard Packwood

"It is a pity that an intelligent creature like the elephant should be shot in order that creatures not much more intelligent may play billiards with balls made from their teeth."

Captain Richard Meinertzhagen, *Kenyan Diary*, 1903

ELEPHANTS have huge appetites. They spend about three-quarters of each day and night gathering trunkful after trunkful of food—up to 500 pounds per day for an adult bull. They are selective feeders, but because the trunk can both smell and touch things at the same time, it can select, pick, and, if need be, prepare each morsel without its owner necessarily looking at the food before it is put into its mouth. The range of food types available to an elephant is unparalleled: By standing up on its hind legs, an elephant with outstretched trunk can reach leaves higher than a giraffe. By shaking the whole tree, an elephant can bring ripe fruit down to the ground. By tusking the earth, roots and tubers can be dug up. And by wading out into the swamps, lush grasses can be gathered.

THERE ARE three main feeding bouts each day—during the morning, in the afternoon, and in the middle of the night—with

Ardea London John Wightman

Frank Lane Picture Agency Ltd

time in between for digestion and other activities. During the heat of the day, elephants will seek shade and relax, but the main rest period is in the early hours of the morning before dawn. Elephants fall into a deep sleep for between one and four hours each night, often

snoring contentedly. Very large elephants may sleep standing up, but most lie down on one side.

Elephants have a thirst that is almost equal to their appetite for food, but they usually visit water only once or twice each day. The trunk is used to lift water to the mouth, but not like a drinking straw. Each draught is drawn up into the trunk, then the end of the trunk is shut tight and curled into the mouth. The elephant then tilts its head back, opens its trunk, and lets the water gush down its throat. Skin care is another daily activity. This involves a combination of bathing (using the trunk as a built-in shower attachment), dusting, plastering with mud, and scratching. Bathing is both a means of keeping cool and of keeping the skin soft and supple. A bath is often

followed by a mud pack or a thorough dusting, which prolongs the cooling period and acts as a sunscreen to protect the skin from sunburn. Layers of dried

Hugo Van Lawick/Nature Photographers Ltd

Ardea London Jim & Julie Bruton

mud and dead skin are later rubbed off against a tree trunk or a conveniently shaped boulder. Elephants are among that elite group of animals that can make and use tools, and if an itch is in an awkward place, a stick may be grasped in the trunk and used to scratch it.

Dieter Plage/Survival Anglia

ONE OF THE most moving and mysterious facets of elephant behavior is the way they treat their dead. Elephants show a strong interest in the remains of deceased elephants—particularly of late relatives—whether they have died recently or some years before. They slowly feel over the body or skeleton with the trunk tip, as if recalling the individual they once knew, and will often pick up and scatter old bones and tusks.

Kyle Owens, who was working in Burkina Faso in 1986, witnessed a remarkable scene. While watching a herd of eight elephants with a tiny baby, he saw the baby was ill. Throughout the morning the mother tried everything to raise the calf to its feet. "She dropped to her knees and lifted the baby with her trunk. She gently rocked him to an upright position with her forefoot. Each time the baby fell back onto his side with a scream, and each time the mother screamed too . . . the frustration, hope, and suffering brought tears to my eyes.

"At dusk I returned. The baby had died. His tiny body was barely visible as the other elephants had covered him with dirt, grass, and leaves. The mother positioned herself over her child and began to rock. Occasionally another elephant would stroke her back affectionately, or intertwine trunks, but she continued to rock as darkness fell."

Another zoologist, Dr. J. "Hezy" Shoshani, was visiting Amboseli in Kenya with friends. "We came across the carcass of an elephant, and a female with her calf was standing nearby. They moved into the bushes and we stopped to take a look at the decomposing body. I began to cut a small section of skin to show my students, when suddenly the female appeared from the bushes, spread her ears, and charged from about fifteen paces!" The resulting confusion was comical in

Jonathan Scott/Planet Earth Pictures

"It was a ceremony, a funeral of sorts. A complex and intricate ritual conducted by elephants in honor of their fallen brother. The experience will be with me forever as a constant reminder of the magnificence, intelligence, and compassion of elephants."

Kyle Owens

retrospect, but the point of the story is more profound. The female resumed her position standing over the body; she had made them realize that it wasn't just a dead elephant lying there. It was a living elephant's dead relative or friend.

Ian Redmond

*T*HE CRISIS now facing each species of elephant represents the final stages of a process that began thousands of years ago. It is no exaggeration to say that elephants were once the dominant species throughout most of Africa and southern Asia. Elephants lived almost everywhere, outnumbering by far the scattered tribes of *Homo sapiens.* During the period of recorded history, however, elephant numbers and range have steadily declined as a direct result of human activity.

Much of Africa and Asia is now a cultivated landscape, crisscrossed by roads and fences and dotted with modern cities. There are still islands of elephants in this sea of humanity, but these are rapidly shrinking in the face of an expanding human population.

Every rural family wants its little patch of land to cultivate, but it is often said that one cannot share an acre with an elephant. In terms of temperature, rainfall, and soil fertility, elephants have the same sort of requirements as humans. As a result, elephants are steadily being evicted from their former range, which they later visit—an activity that people call "crop raiding." This loss of habitat presents the greatest long-term threat to elephant survival, but the network of parks and reserves would be enough to save the species *if* the poaching could be stopped.

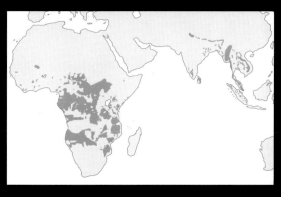

The present, scattered distribution of elephant populations in Africa and Asia.

"Why don't they just let the elephants die of old age? Then their tusks will be bigger and they can just pick them up off the ground without shooting."

Matthew Gamble,
Eight-year-old schoolboy

Philip Cayford

$\mathcal{T}$HE IVORY TRADE is illogical. Complex computer models of trade data have confirmed what is obvious to a child—the most profitable way of managing elephants is to let them die of old age. This is because, to the carvers of luxury ornaments in Japan, ivory from large tusks is worth more per pound than the same weight made up of small tusks; also, old elephants have already reproduced and passed on their wisdom to the next generation. A herd of elephants is the nearest thing in real life to the fairy-tale goose that laid the golden egg.

Before the ban, up to 94 percent of the trade in ivory stemmed from poaching, even if the tusks were recovered by rangers and then sold legally. Driven by an apparently insatiable demand for ivory and the desire for instant profits, the poachers were killing elephants of all ages and both sexes. This is reflected in the trade statistics. The ivory trade grew steadily between 1950—when 224 tons of tusks were sold—and 1983, when the figure was 1,100 tons. The annual total then began to fall: 660 tons in 1986; 330 tons in 1987. But this did not mean that fewer elephants were being killed. In 1979, one ton of ivory represented about fifty-nine dead elephants— mainly bulls with large tusks

declined. But the fact that poaching is reported to rise in the least protected areas each time the ivory ban is reviewed suggests that there is no room for complacency. To some people, killing an elephant is tantamount to murder. To others it is a tempting passport to riches.

(average weight: 21.5 pounds). By 1987, most mature bulls had been shot, and so the cows and calves were being killed for their smaller tusks (average weight: 10.3 pounds). Thus, one ton of ivory in 1987 came from about 124 dead elephants, many of them adult females whose calves (with no ivory) were orphaned and left to die of starvation.

One thing was clear from these statistics. If we did not voluntarily end the ivory trade, the trade would end itself by wiping out the source of its raw material.

Now that ivory is no longer fashionable in much of the world, the trade has

*I*N ASIA the elephant is venerated. Domestic elephants still play a role in carrying timber and tourists through the forests, and as the bearers of royalty or religious relics in processions. But only 35,000—55,000 Asian elephants survive in the wild, plus about 16,000 in captivity. And unlike any other domestic animal, each new generation is captured from the wild and trained. As numbers dwindle, such captures now threaten the survival of some wild herds.

Is it possible for humans and elephants to coexist peacefully? In the very heart of Africa, on the shores of a lake, lies a fishing village called Vitshumb. It is located in the Virunga National Park, Congo (formerly Zaire). Before the civil war, villagers and elephants were so tolerant of each other that the elephants would wander down the main street and quietly forage for kitchen waste while children played nearby.

Sadly, those elephants have been badly hit by the ivory gangs, but the principle remains. Where there is no conflict, humans *can* live alongside elephants. Thanks to the rise in ecotourism, elephants are worth more alive than dead. Land set aside for elephants can earn more than almost any other form of land use. Kenya is visited by up to 900,000 adult tourists each year, bringing in hundreds of millions of dollars—there is no doubt that elephants are one of the main attractions. Thus elephants play a central role in the economy as well as the ecology of the countries they inhabit. They are the flagship of the wildlife conservation movement. If we cannot save the elephants, what hope is there for the lesser creatures whose fate rests in our hands?

Ardea London *Julie Bartlett*

"I first saw elephants in their natural habitat when my father took me to Africa in 1946. They were altogether different from their sad relatives confined to circuses and zoos.

So abundant were the herds, I could hardly have imagined that one day I would be involved in international efforts to save them from extinction."

Prince Sadruddin Aga Khan,
President, The Bellerive Foundation

After its launch in May 1989, ELEFRIENDS rapidly grew into a major conservation movement. Now part of the Born Free Foundation, it is supported by more than a million people, including many internationally known celebrities and politicians. The ELEFRIENDS Project had two objectives—to support effective antipoaching in the field and to tackle the consumer markets for ivory around the world. It has now added a third—to seek ways of reducing conflict between elephants and people.

Overall, elephant numbers continue to fall—probably fewer than 400,000 in Africa and 40,000 in the wild in Asia remain—although in well-protected areas they are increasing. This leads to the paradox of too many elephants in small, fenced, protected areas and the need for a humane method of controlling their numbers. Some argue that the costs of protecting elephants should be met by the sale of the legally acquired ivory. However, as long as ivory is traded as a commodity, there will be poachers willing to devastate the remaining herds where protection is weakest. It is up to us to persuade consumers all around the world that ivory, far from being desirable, is the product of a sickening, cruel mass slaughter.

With the support of ELEFRIENDS everywhere, the Born Free Foundation now supports antipoaching initiatives in a number of African countries, community wildlife programs, the production of education materials (both printed and online), and continued monitoring of the ivory trade. Please help us.

For further information, please write to **ELEFRIENDS, Born Free Foundation, 3 Grove House, Foundry Lane, Horsham, RH13 5PL, England.** Or visit the Born Free Foundation website: **www.bornfree.org.uk**

Asian elephants 10, 13, 25, 46

Baby elephants *see calves*
Bathing 23, 39
Bull elephants 6, 8, 13, 27, 28, 29, 30, 31, 33, 36, 45
Bush elephants 8, 13, 17, 18

Calves 4, 6, 23, 25, 26, 31, 32—33, 35, 36—37, 45
Cave elephants 6, 25
Communication 8, 12, 26, 28, 30, 31

Death 5, 6, 40—41 *see also extinction*
Desert elephants 21
Digging 10, 18, 21, 24, 38
Dusting 39

Ears 8, 12, 13, 14, 18, 26, 35, 40
Ecology 8, 18, 46
Estrus 27, 30, 31
Extinction 4, 6, 46—47
Eyelashes 12
Eyes 12

Family 26, 30, 31, 35, 36, 37, 40
Feet 15, 31, 40

Female elephants 4, 8, 10, 25, 26, 27, 28, 30, 31, 32, 35, 36, 37, 40, 45
Fighting 28, 29, 36
Food 17, 18, 26, 32, 33, 38—39
Forest elephants 6, 13, 18

Greeting ceremony 26, 27

Hair 14
Hunting 4, 5, 28

Ivory 4, 5, 6, 7, 44, 45, 46

Matriarch 26—27, 36
Musth 13, 28, 29, 31, 33, 36

National parks 4, 6, 46

Orphans 4, 45

Playing 23, 35, 36
Poaching 4, 6, 28, 43, 44—45, 46

Salt 24, 25
Skin 14, 23, 39
Sleeping 38, 39

Tail 14, 26
Teeth 6, 7, 10, 17, 24 *see also tusks*
Temporal gland 13, 28, 31
Threat display 10, 35
Trunk 10, 11, 12, 14, 21, 24, 30, 31, 32, 35, 38, 39, 40
Tusks 4, 6, 10, 18, 21, 24, 25, 36, 38, 40, 44, 45

Washing 23, 39
Water 18, 21, 23, 39

Oxford Scientific Films
Richard Packwood